Flame Shoulder Moth

poems by

Diana Deering

Finishing Line Press
Georgetown, Kentucky

Flame Shoulder Moth

But when the door shuts on us, all that vanishes. The shell-like covering which our souls have excreted to house themselves, to make for themselves a shape distinct from others, is broken, and there is left of all these wrinkles and roughnesses a central oyster of perceptiveness, an enormous eye.

—Virginia Woolf, "Street Haunting"

Copyright © 2019 by Diana Deering
ISBN 978-1-64662-093-7 First Edition
All rights reserved under International and Pan-American Copyright Conventions. No part of this book may be reproduced in any manner whatsoever without written permission from the publisher, except in the case of brief quotations embodied in critical articles and reviews.

ACKNOWLEDGMENTS

To the countless in the trenches medical professionals who quietly, steadfastly give their lives to their work. To those who have touched mine: especially Ann Cutcher, Carol Maynard, Sigrid Lonnberg, Pam Miller, Patricia Cable and Naomi Lev for their love and support.
Thank you to Judith Vollmer, Mihaela Moscauliuc and Sarah Vap for generously reading and responding to this manuscript, & whose wise guidance helped me trust the shape of these poems. To my Drew community of poets. To Joe Stroud whose early teaching and love of poetry set me on my way. To my family and friends, especially Lorraine Healy, Sharon Shoemaker, Elisa Miller, Susan Berg, Cynthia Adams and Bernice Rendrick for their unwavering encouragement. To Susan Scott and Grace McLeod for their vision. To SDB, always.

I borrow from these writers' texts with deep respect and admiration; their words gave me the courage to speak.

Publisher: Leah Maines
Editor: Christen Kincaid
Cover Art: Susan Burgers
Author Photo: Susan Burgers
Cover Design: Elizabeth Maines McCleavy

Printed in the USA on acid-free paper.
Order online: www.finishinglinepress.com
       also available on amazon.com

Author inquiries and mail orders:
Finishing Line Press
P. O. Box 1626
Georgetown, Kentucky 40324
U. S. A.

Table of Contents

I. for the nurses
"In fluorescent hallways…" 1
"What I once called truth…" 2
"What is losing…" 3
"When the hospital administrator…" 4
"To implicate…" 5
"When my friends say…" 6
"But absolutely necessary…" 7
"When the woman…" 8
"When he was peeling…" 9
"The tread of tires…" 10
"Are you there…" 11
"Moth there is rage…" 12
"Moth you come at night…" 13
"Break plates…" 14
"Dazed from my…" 15
"Where does the spirit…" 16
"There are many ways…" 17

II. devotions
"The heart roams…" 18
"Moth I have been dodging" 19
"Moth in the dream…" 20
"She said our memory…" 21
"I drop the letter…" 22
"I walk out…" 23
"I am indebted…" 24
"I peer inside…" 25
"Scratch paper, post-its…" 26
"Echo, prism, rescue…" 27
"Silk flecked with…" 28

III. whistling over tundra
"For those who are made…" 29
"Moth you give up…" 30
"A thousand yards…" 31
"What is the sound…" 32
"It is a children's story…" 33
"One hollow rib…" 34

Coda 35
Bio

I. for the nurses

In fluorescent hallways
their shadows pass before the windows,
a clipped beating my feet remember

before the midnight stations:
sickness, old age, death, birth.
She said *it is a fact that is inside you.*

I would shout up to them *Sisters!*
sealed behind glass,
absorbed in their hourly rounds.

Destined, called, urgently needed—
It is a fact that is inside you
what you have touched.

I. for the nurses

What I once called truth,
There are many kinds of mourning.

Flame floods the shoulders now,
the membrane between fire and ice
two realms of burning.

Stars hang paralyzed
the sun reverses course.

Hildegard said *part of the terror
is to take back our listening.*

We cannot live in a world interpreted by others.
The arms want to heal.

She said *these visions which I saw
were not in sleep nor in dreams,
not by eye or external ears.*[1]

---

1 Hildegard von Bingen (1098-1171) German Benedictine abbess, writer, composer, herbalist, visionary

I. for the nurses

What is losing moth? Tell me what is loss. Celan said *Listen your way in with your mouth*.[2] I am running down hallways, in buildings without doors. How does the body emerge out of sleeplessness? The attorney advised me to settle. A hundred thousand dollars for a hearing and even then I might lose. This is what happened to me. He said *insurmountable when we're awake, we sleep across, up to the Gates of Mercy*.[3] There are those who, like him, throw themselves into rivers. There are mothers lifting children out. The mouths of fishes face up. He said *I let the heart/ I had / hope*[4]

---

2 "*listen your way in*" Paul Celan, (John Felstiner, *Poet, Survivor, Jew*, Yale, 1995)
3 "*insurmountable...*" Paul Celan ("Die Poles/ The Poles", *Paul Celan, Poems*, trans Michael Hamburger, Persea Books, 1980)
4 "*I let the heart...*" Paul Celan ("Zurich, Zum Storchen"/ "Zurich, To the Storks", Ibid)

I. for the nurses

When the hospital administrator said I should ask for forgiveness, I asked her to repeat herself thinking I had misheard, but she chanted like a priest. She would administer the sacraments. Racing in place, zooming out, I saw the plan being executed: script pre-ordained, signed off and not a word edgewise. A religion not baptized to but nonetheless subjected. God have mercy. Christ have mercy. The call calculated to end abruptly without reassurance. I was to discuss the incident with no one, remain off work indefinitely. In deprivation experiments a monkey is placed in a stainless-steel trough without a source of light for up to ten weeks. At first it will exhibit signs of panic, but within a few days will have stopped moving and remain huddled in a corner. I sat in my car, an insect pinging against glass, little breaths of flame, but frozen. Kindergarten teachers taught us to poke holes in the lid, even then I couldn't bear it.

I. for the nurses

To implicate, to fold or twist together, by withholding facts, to convey indirectly through what one says, rather than stating explicitly; to imply. To involve as a consequence, to bring into incriminating connection. Often for the purposes of relieving personal responsibility or involvement, to discharge or unburden.

For each will have to bear his own load. Each will give an account of himself to God.[5]
He said *Therefore let us not judge nor put obstacles in another's way.* She said it was law: egg, caterpillar, pupa, moth. *Inevitable as that which swings suns, moons and planets in their courses.*[6] He said *every living being—trees, plants, insects—all have independent characteristics, energy and power.*[7] That day I fell in front of the dryer, a guttural sound coming from my throat. Was that when you first heard me moth.

---

5 *"For each will have to bear..."* (Romans, 14:13)
6 *"Inevitable as that which swings..."* (Gene-Stratton-Porter, *Moths of the Limberlost*, Doubleday, 1912) p. 25
7 *"every living being..."* (Kilung Rinpoche, South Whidbey Record, May 24, 2017)

I. for the nurses

When my friends say *Get Angry!* I want to reply: If you're an animal in a trap you move warily to avoid teeth digging further into the ankle. You learn to play dead, breathe with the least oscillation possible, steady as the line of water in a glass. Blood courses the ears, you cannot help but hear it pound. Cell walls lift and lower their gates. Mostly dead ends, but under flood lights for you moth, no locks. I want to say the exhaustion of capture is such.

I. for the nurses

But *absolutely necessary to speak of, however incoherently, she said language was incommensurate with it.*[8]
When they look away, gather their things,
vertigo, loss of altitude, plummet, are you bewildered moth, are you lonely?
She said *the black hole and the imperative to tell. A vanishing point. The fear that fate will strike again, fear of being listened to— and of listening to yourself.*[9]

Close the shades, sip in the dark.

---

8 "*absolutely necessary to speak of...*" Shoshana Felman (Testimony, Crisis in Witnessing in Literature, Psychoanalysis, and History, Routledge, 1992) p. 50
9 "*black hole and the imperative to tell...*" "*The fear...*" (Ibid) p. 65

I. for the nurses

When the woman grabs her child in a crowded supermarket aisle and turns away (a commotion of shopping carts, drawn in breath), does she believe me contaminated moth, does she presume to know me, is it a shunning? Wilderness, without exit. Am I ten, pressed against a locker, nipples chafing inside a borrowed bathing suit or hairless as the litter of rabbits you uncovered under the peonies, eyes still sealed, no mother in sight.

I. for the nurses

When he was peeling an avocado at the kitchen sink and said what is happening with your nursing license, along the fence I saw leaf points caught in a slow motion flap of breeze, little pointed flags like those you might see on a castle in Wales, as he went on about the accusation and blacklisting, could it be possible? do these things really happen? as though speaking to himself only, in theory, in abstraction. the shame of it all, shame, shame, shame. I said nothing, could not move.

I. for the nurses

There is the tread of tires left in a field but this is invisible. court doors are soundless.
briefcases, witness stand, judge, raise your right hand for emotional truth. a pulse stacatto's the neck until the roaring becomes wind or soundless. what is the code to the bathroom, what pounds then slivers like glass. worse than hatred which may be a perversion of love, indifference is said to be most agonizing.

I. for the nurses

Are you there as I utter my responses, briefcases already snapped shut. Decided, absconded, predetermined, filed in writing, contracted and paid, advised to do so. In airless rooms you listen in vents, air conditioning ducts, fire sprinklers on stucco ceilings, intercoms. Robbers, thieves moth: to take the property of others, to come and go secretly, to take by force or unjust means, to accomplish in a concealed or unobserved manner. She said *the answers to a set of hostile questions, in the attempt to wear down her resistance and trick her into perjuring herself. Truth was never what her judges sought.*[10] To *get rid of,* throw away, shed, dispose of, do away with, eliminate, dump. eradicate, dispense with. **a:** To cover up: a device or stratagem for masking or concealing **b:** a usually concerted effort to keep an illegal or unethical act or situation from being made public.

When I pass there again, my heart beats faster because what happened there was a deception, a sacrifice.

---

10 *"the answers to a set of hostile questions…"* Kathryn Harrison (*Joan Of Arc, A Life Transfigured*, Random House, 2014)

I. for the nurses

Moth, there is rage. A nest of scorpions for the warden's bed. To lie: to make an untrue statement with intent to deceive. To pleasure at instilling fear. Moth, you are sweating. Blinds, lure, flashing lights to confuse, plastic nocturnal flowers, the glow of your thirst. Beware of those who trust only themselves, and treat others with contempt. Moth, you are panting. Steer clear. They are not your people or your moths.

I. for the nurses

Moth you come at night for privacy, for coolness. Administer to the throat. Windowsill & door jam. He said *the divine in the absence of the human, until the human could make itself known.*[11] To dedicate oneself to. Through peep-holes we sound out the words. Mouth their treacheries: *complaint, allegation, accusation, charge*: sizzle and froth on the tongue. Syllables for which there are no pictures. Celan said *the language with which I make my poems has nothing to do with the one spoken here.*[12] She said *an effort was required to arouse myself to realize I was not dreaming.*[13] What does it mean moth to hang in the balance of words? To hold burning alphabets and not bury, not catch fire. To refuse. Ionesco said *How can you be revealed by what hides you? All that remains for me to do is to give the lie to each spoken word by taking it apart, by making it explode.*[14] Moth you said libel, defamation. When my attorney asked the hospital administrator: Did you disparage my client to this family? She flushed and averted her eyes. He said a poem is not information. A poem is not an argument. You don't have to translate yourself. To the boys who set fire to cars to revel in the blast, for another destroying outside the self, for the physical release, I will not blame them.

---

11 *"the divine in the absence..."* Donald Kalschcd (*Trauma and the Soul*, Routledge, 2013) p. 9
12 *" the language with which I make my poems..."* Paul Celan (from a letter to his wife from Germany)
13 *"an effort was required..."* Gene-Stratton-Porter (Ibid.)
14 *"how can you be revealed..."* Eugene Ionesco (*Present Past, Past Present*, trans. Helen Lane, Grove Press)

I. for the nurses

Break plates for the din, gash, schism, rupture, for jaggedness, for escape. Launch, pelt, pitch, hurl moth, crash, splintering. Shatter. For time and recurrence, for fire, repercussions, because of what happens to people, incomprehensible, because of randomness, because of evil.

I. for the nurses

Dazed from my mother's hospitalization, I drive home to collect a toothbrush, clean socks. A fugue state. An earthworm stretches in front of the door. She said a poem is not an argument. *A doctrine of correspondences.*[15] How do you arrive in the body of another? As evidence. To startle out of. To reveal or confirm. When I was six, I lifted their pearl-grey bodies off the flooded driveway, carried them to earth. A pact or for their willingness, their silk in my palms. She said *bearers of secret wisdom, every chance encounter,*[12] already a template of your whisper moth.

---

15 "*a doctrine of correspondences*" "*bearers of secret wisdom*", Melissa Kwasny, (from "Learning to Speak With Them" and " God Step at the Margins of Thought", *Earth Recitals, Essays on Image and Vision*, Lynx House Press, 2013) p. 18

I. for the nurses

Where does the spirit go? All day the dying goldfish labors upside down, its tail a battered dress, thrashing silver underbelly, the seam of its locket. He said *search for the soul's release in language.*[16] I mouth through the glass, you are not alone in your suffering. I've seen dying people lift their whole rib cage for a single breath, cheeks sucked in. Soon after I got the notice, she came home with two goldfish circling in a tied off plastic bag. Then every human was a razor. Condolences, love the most searing. But you goldfish, speechless and suspended too. Were you speaking with your eyes?

---

16 *"search for the soul's release..",* Ilya Kaminski (from an interview with Philip Metres, American Poetry Review, March/April 2017)

I. for the nurses

There are many ways of travel. You thrum under the moon, ears buried in your abdomen. Carrier, escape, you navigate by maintaining a constant relationship to a bright celestial object. Your hearing is the most sensitive in the animal kingdom, adapted to the clicks of bats. There is no one who believes you. Blow out through all sides of the ribs. Go still as leaves. Belong under dresses without poison, on lamp shades, in keyholes. The world is not finished yet.

II. devotions

The heart roams the hospital lobby moth. Mission statement: *We honor the dignity of every person. All people are created in the image of God. (Genesis 1:27)* Where will I go? Where is my flower? I bump through corridors, blindfolded by instinct, pollen's mother tongue. She said the poem will tell you what is next. I walk, a ghost but not disembodied, a figure inside a shadow. Eurydice paced her underground chambers sealed beneath a heavy peat door. He called it *a second world,* he said *where the personal story is interrupted the archetypal story begins.* Gift shop, bronze plaque of donors, cancer center. Citizen, badge-less, worse than expulsion: un-chosen. Moth help me. He said *this resonant image provided a story, a matrix of two worlds that kept her soul in being.*[17]

---

17 *"a second world...where the personal story is interrupted..."* and *"this resonant image..."* Donald Kalsched, (*Trauma and the Soul,* Routledge, 2013) p. 50

II. devotions

Moth, I have been dodging your messages spooled between midnight and three a.m., a ceaseless fluttering. Am I sleeping or awake? Your white eggs dot careful rows inside the watering pail. You confide in oak bark and the underside of bridges, in days you will be gone. She said *what divine thought flowering in the world of spirit.*[15] So many doors moth, so many layers. Five successive skins, seven months as you digest your self. What survives? Stencils of eyes, wings, antennae. Nerves. Forethoughts, imaginal discs. Imago. She said *it is a threshold to whatever meaning it has and a door. It must not reveal everything; it must leave something for us to find.*[18] It was an extreme physiological need akin to sleep, something that could not be refused. She said *time sense may be altered, often with a sense of slow motion and the experience may lose its quality of ordinary reality.*[19] Look how you proceed, look how you are bound! Keep faith with your vision! I am paralyzed. Watch over me. I will keep my promise. I will honor your devotions.

---

18 *"what divine thought..." "it is a threshold..."* Adonis (Sufism and Surrealism, as quoted by Melissa Kwasny, Ibid) p. 130
19 *"time sense may be altered..."* Judith Herman (*Trauma and Recovery*, Basic Books, 1992) p.43

II. devotions

Moth, in the dream I am lifting a patient, pillows to support the arms, clean linens
he has vomited, oxygen, Morphine, Lorazepam, call the family, call his wife Dorothy.

> Occupation: A person's work or business, especially as a means of making a living; vocation: a summons or strong inclination: as a sense of who a person is or where she is going, an inner voice. He said *we make a pilgrimage with our labors.*[20]

> *The removal of the old identity and temporary assumption of a nonidentity.*[21] *You will be caught in fearful places that make no sense.*[22] "Another common aspect of the participants' callings was the experience of a unique intensity, specifically they reported a heightened degree of ease, energized focus, being fully immersed, or even a spiritual presence when completing tasks."[23]

Was that you moth? In hallways, at bedsides, night shift day evening at my wrist, wafer-like, rustling?

---

20 *"we make a pilgrimage..."* David Whyte (*Crossing the Unknown Sea, Work as a Pilgrimage of Identity,* Riverhead Books, 2001) p. 5
21 *"the removal of an old identity..."* William Bridges (*Transitions,* Da Capo, 2001)116
22 *"fearful places that make no sense"* William Bridges, Ibid.) p.184
23 *another common aspect..."* Jared French (from *Life Calling and Vocation,* PhD thesis, Trinity Western University, 2006)

II. devotions

She said *our memory repeats to us what we haven't understood.*[24]
It is like something you memorized once and forgot[25]

Lepidoptera
The way a river is once only a dreaming in snow
before the multiple surrenders.

---

24 "*our memory repeats to us*" Valery ("*Commentaire de Charmes*", Oeuvres, Paris, 1957)
25 "*it is like something you memorized...*" Annie Dilliard (*The Writing Life*, HarperCollins, 1989) p.76

II. devotions

I drop the letter into the box at Broadway and 14th. An act of faith, one leftover Virgin and Child Christmas stamp affixed. Celan said *the poem is lonely. It is lonely and en route.*[26] He said *a poem is a message in a bottle that may or may not be found.*[27] By momentum, by wishes, by nightfall it may breach the Rockies, cross over bears in torpid slumber, pulse so whispered they are unreachable now. Elk are dark holes, fish slide under glass, salamanders open and close their gills before thaw. Day and night the umbilical tug. He called it *the sound of the dark.* He said *it is in fact the spirit of the earth.*[28]

---

26 *"the poem is lonely.."* Paul Celan (Meridian speech, 1960)
27 *"the poem is a message…"* Paul Celan (Ibid)
28 *"the sound of the dark…"* Federico Garcia-Lorca ("The Theory and Play of the Duende" 1933, *In Search of Duende*, New Directions, 1975)

II. devotions

I walk out of the hospital's double doors into neighborhoods, hood over my head, it is still winter. There are other moons, I must learn about them. A child wrestles with his dog, a father carries groceries to a back door. A bike beside. Other satellites moth, differing tides and calendars. New imperatives. How does the soul wish? Not thirsty, desperate in its affections, nor punishing in its reward. Total strangers tell me *be seen*, a teabag tag says *be heard*, in the waiting room a headline proclaims new proof of *the power of the healing encounter*. She said *a coincidence that is almost uncanny*,[29] beyond any reductive psychological trivialization. Thinking in terms of the whole he said it is not magic, a divination. Instead there may be a dimension of meaning that apparently exists outside man.[30] I will take a chance on it. It is not a contest, not a performance, you said *it will happen whether or not you okay it.*

---

29 "*a coincidence that is almost uncanny*" (*Testimony*, Ibid.)
30 "*thinking in terms of the whole...*" Carl Jung ("Synchronicity, An Acausal Principle", 1952)

II. devotions

I am indebted to you moth, your byways and scholarship, bright blue devotions in the Philadelphus, your absolute vow. Speechless, bereft, I rifle your archive, pickpocket your collections. To testify to inner voices. Under the cover of night you deliver your sheaves. A tumult, an embarrassment of riches: tragedy, brilliance, testimony. The events of a life. He called it *the complicate*.[31] Not an explanation. She said. *I was looking desperately for clues*,[32] *trying to find metaphoric equivalents.*[33]

---

31 "*the complicate*" Wallace Stevens ("Notes Toward a Supreme Fiction", 1962)
32 "*I was looking desperately for clues, because if there were no clues I thought I might be insane.*" Adrienne Rich ("When We Dead Reawaken: Writing as Revision", Ibid.) p.44
33 "*...trying to find metaphoric equivalents...*" (Sandra Gilbert and Susan Gubar, describing Emily Dickinson in *Madwoman in the Attic*, Yale, 1979) p.585

II. devotions

I peer inside silk tents. Hundreds drape in vertical rungs, slack after a day of foraging. The woods crackle not unlike fire. What are the categories of silence? They said we will proceed with the charges as they were assigned. Poetry is for the wound not the torturer. Propelled, the caterpillars labor across blacktop knowing nothing of cars. What are the chances? You said it yourself, even the unlucky cannot be wholly captured, the soul will not allow it. When no one is looking they enter their sacs, bind their bodies in cloth, prepare for metamorphosis.

II. devotions

Scratch paper, post-its, airports, trains, taxi, back seats, pencils lost and found, notebooks, legal pads. Discovery. Doubt. Questions without answers, an equivalent chaos. You persist moth, won't let go. Fly into doctor's offices, family dinners, courtrooms, two deaths and my mother's bedside. A pillow for my weariness, a peripheral vision. What are your timetables? That day I woke in utter blackness, began the antidepressant. She said *but poems are like dreams: in them you put what you don't know you know.*[34] An emergency to mark, resist erasure. She said *the arrival as a point of departure for another kind of journey.*[35]

---

34 "*but poems are like dreams*" Adrienne Rich (*On Lies, Secrets and Silence*, Norton, 1979) p. 40
35 "*arrival as a point of departure*" (*Testimony*, Ibid) p. 255

II. devotions

Echo, prism, rescue, a constellation of texts, a record moth, a document. Research, investigation, sources. Homage. Unearth, decipher. He said *Too feeble for such flights were my own wings.*[36] Poets, mystics, sages, I scrawl their sentences, drink their magnitudes. Without hoax. Celan: *poems are making toward something standing open, occupiable, perhaps toward a 'thou' that can be addressed, an addressable reality.*[37] She said *I think a certain kind of believing abandon to poetry can bring about what seems a miracle.*[38]

---

36 *"too feeble..."*, Dante Alighieri, *The Divine Comedy*, Paradiso 33, 137-145 translation L.G. White, Pantheon, 1948
37 *"poems are making toward.."* Paul Celan, (Bremen speech, 1958)
38 *"I think a certain kind of believing..."* Denise Levertov (from "Notes on Organic Form", *the poet in the world,* New Directions, 1960, p. 229)

II. devotions

Silk flecked with chewed bark, leaf, mud,
unspools from holes in your jaw.
Cloak, bury, wrap, in order to dissolve.
He said *we have died many times and in many places.*[39]
Lepidoptera—
*Or we might liken it to a mirror; or to a kaleidoscope
gifted with consciousness,*[40]
your thorax will become the hinge for two doors

---

39 "*We have died many times…*" Meister Eckhat (I.M. Oderberg, Meister Eckhart: Friend of God, *Sunrise Magazine*, Theosophical University Press, December1989/ January 1990)
40 "*Or we might liken it to a mirror…*", Charles Baudelaire (from "*The Painter of Modern Life and Other Essays*", Phaidon Press, 1985)

III. Whistling over tundra

For those who are made mute
the soul is ferried in the medium of others.
Because of helplessness we steel ourselves.
Eight months, you progress through your stages
to secrete eggs on a branch.
Your manifesto and prophecy. Don't let me
die not having spoken.
Show me my branch.

III. Whistling over tundra

Moth you give up sky for sealed conference rooms, flying for derailment. What are your obligations? Who are your grandmothers? Single minded, you swift pollen through dusk. Crowd under street lights. How do you choose your elixirs, summon your ecstasies? He said *A multiplicity of voices enveloped in a single narrative.*[41] The poem you want to write is not what you think, it will disarm you, approach at midnight moth, enclose you in its spell.

---

41 "*a multiplicity of voices...*" William Kentridge and Rosalind C. Morris (*that which is not drawn*, Seagull Books, 2017) p. 44

III. Whistling over tundra

A thousand yards, three days to spin your enclosure. Your head swings in figure eights. Where are you going moth? Where are you drawn? Your absolute seclusion, insulate, cell. Seven days to a year without food or water. What are your requirements? What is your singing? She said *something vast, irreducible, a spirit summoned by the needing and the making*.[42] To split your skin, free the underneath.

---

42 Denise Levertov, *the poet in the world*, "Origins of a Poem" (New Directions, 1960) p. 47

III. Whistling over tundra

What is the sound of wind moth? Whistling over tundra at break up, parting the fur of rabbits as they dart under workers' shacks, beneath the 126 million year old Brooks range. Is it breath, salmon ribs winnowed in the Nooksack and Stillaguamish after the run. Silver and battered, the muscled fin a salty parchment. Once under the circling eye of eagles, I saw them thrash, laboring to the ground of their birth. As a child I thought it was a haunting, voices or water. Is it instinct, north, gravity of snows and a thousand unnamed islands between here and there where guillemots roost in rocky cavities and the rasp of terns chastens the air. Summer solstice but already an inner sleeve of ice.

III. Whistling over tundra

A children's story, a glued handmade thing: mend, thread, stitch, knot. Curse, riddle, lullaby. Lament. Innocence, wound, paper's torn and fluid edge. Your promise, your customs clammer in my chest. She said *the poem is a beautiful voyage not by your own will.*[42]

---

[42] "*the poem is a beautiful voyage…*" Barbara Guest (*Forces of Imagination*, Kelsey Street Press, 2005) p. 79

III. Whistling over tundra

One hollow rib chafes,

memorized to wheels
in corridors, gauze,
tape, skin,

bone.

You said look for the truth
in the crevice of cold rocks.
It will not be what you expect,

it will be colder

and luckier.

Coda:

for nurses, for guardians, for all couriers of healing,

infinitely praised and blamed, remembered or indelibly forgotten

Diana Deering completed an MFA in Poetry at Drew University. This project arose out of her experience of being falsely accused and denied the opportunity to defend herself while working as a nurse. Profoundly shaken, she lost her voice. In an attempt to understand her state, she dove into the literature of trauma. The voices of others revealed a path back to herself. The figure of the moth arrived unexpectedly. A creature outside of the treacherous human realm, not flashy like a butterfly, but plain, dusty grey, unassuming, often disliked, a being that—mostly under the radar—undergoes a profound transformation in the cycle of its life. The moth became a powerful intermediary, a spirit guide and confidant.